Anita is so devoted to the couples she works with and so deeply strives to make things work. Her brilliant creativity has birthed these remarkably creative ways of putting your relationship first. The runway is lit up to making your relationship last.

Howard Glasser, creator of the Nurtured Heart Approach and author of several books, including *Igniting Greatness*.

FIRST COMES US:

The Busy Couple's Guide to Lasting Love

by
Anita A. Chlipala, LMFT

first

comes

US

The Busy Couple's Guide *to lasting love*

ANITA A. CHLIPALA, LMFT   America's Leading
Relationship Therapist

For bulk orders, please email info@firstcomesusbook.com.

Cover design by Lacey Windschitl. Interior layout design by Victor Kore.

Published by Relationship Reality 312.

Library of Congress Control Number: 2016962839

ISBN 978-0-692-81496-3

www.firstcomesusbook.com

Printed In The United States of America.

to

mfh

___

acknowledgments

I would like to thank these special people in my life for their input, encouragement, patience, and unwavering belief in me and my work.

Michelle Brezek, Bernadette Chlipala, Darek Chlipala and Lisa Sirabian, Inez Corona, Jacqueline Crimmins, Jamie and Brian Duncan, Roxanna Elden, Kim Forystek, Brian Howie, Paul and Melissa Johnson, David Klow, Weykyoi Victor Kore, Diana Lebiecki, Elizabeth Morgan, Sarah Suzuki, Renata Szlaga, and Lacey Windschitl.

And to my parents, John and Leokadia Chlipala, I have no words to express my gratitude for all the ways that you have supported me and for being an example of a loving, lasting marriage.

foreword

Discovery has always been such a captivating word because it encompasses both a journey and an outcome, filled with hope and possibilities. Knowing and working with Anita Chlipala has been one of the great discoveries of my professional life. She is as eloquent, passionate, informative, empowering, self-aware, funny, entertaining, and insightful as anyone I have ever met; every day she continues to discover new ways to reach higher in order to reach all of us.

She understands what makes men tick, what women want, and what all of us need on our path to find love and happiness in our hearts and from our partners, each and every day.

This book is a journey of discovery. You will discover yourselves. You will discover each other. You will discover old memories. You will discover a new connection.

You will discover true love.

BRIAN HOWIE, creator of *The Great Love Debate*

introduction

Love never dies a natural death. It dies because we don't know how to replenish its source.
It dies of blindness and errors and betrayals. It dies of illness and wounds;
it dies of weariness, of witherings, of tarnishings.

— ANAÏS NIN

As a relationship coach and therapist, I've spent a good portion of my practice devoted to saving relationships. Initially I was baffled by how couples who were so in love could end up in my office only a few years later, disliking each other, saying hurtful things, and sitting on the brink

of breaking up or divorce.

I've encountered many couples who have struggled to communicate effectively and lack physical and emotional connection. Some of the most common complaints and concerns I have heard:

We used to be great!
We were best friends.
We used to be so happy. What happened to us?
We don't really talk anymore.
We argue all the time.
It's like I'm living with a roommate. We've had sex 3 times in 6 years.
I don't feel like a priority. I feel like I'm last on the list, after the kids and the dog.
I don't feel appreciated. My spouse takes me for granted.
I feel neglected and ignored.

After getting to know my couples and hearing the stories that brought them to me, I realized many of these problems could have been prevented.

ANITA A. CHLIPALA, LMFT

Couples frequently told me that they thought their love would be enough to sustain their relationship, and that they believed their partner would always be there. They were puzzled as to how their relationship got to the point of such disconnection.

Again and again the answer was simple—a lack of prioritizing the relationship. Given today's demands on our time, it takes conscious effort to put a relationship first. Without it, my couples had fallen into traps that whittled away at their love. This book teaches couples how to put their relationship first in a year's worth of easy-to-do ways that will protect their love, because it needs to be nurtured in order to thrive.

As I found myself reiterating the same advice, giving the same tools, and helping couples with the same problems, I knew I needed a way to reach more couples outside of my office. This book is based on the information I find myself giving to couples most often. In the following pages, I will provide you with the tools to stay connected to your partner. If your relationship is already in a great place, this book will give you the right tools to keep it satisfying and sexy.

first *comes* **US:** The Busy Couple's Guide *to lasting love*

A Better Reality

In order for this book to work, you must believe that your relationship deserves to be the priority in your life. Whether you're reading this and want to bridge the distance between you and your partner, or you want to strengthen the connection you already have, a healthy relationship has to be nurtured every day. Your relationship will be stronger with daily attention. Each day you have healthy and unhealthy choices to make about your relationship—how you respond to each other, whether you allow negative thoughts about your partner to fester, or if you give each other attention even if it is only a quick text, phone call, or hug. Even if you do not have the time to carve out an hour or two every day, there are plenty of brief interactions that can make a huge difference.

You may be saying to yourself, "With everything else I have to do, when will I find the time?" This book was designed with the busy couple in mind. If you're like some of my clients, a relationship book has been on your nightstand, unread, for months. I've picked the most important areas

ANITA A. CHLIPALA, LMFT

4

to strengthen your relationship and addressed them through quick tips and reflections. I don't want you to waste your precious time reading—I want you spending time with your partner.

A Note to Those Who Have Children

Many of the parents in my practice put their children first. You have to put your relationship first—children do better when their parents do better. In fact, every person I have met whose parents put their marriage first said, "I want a marriage like that." The couples who prioritized their children over their marriages are in my office with a vast emotional distance between them. I'm not saying this is easy—even my clients had some initial misgivings and guilt. But the bottom line is that your children will be happier and healthier when you are happier and healthier.

This Feels Forced. Will It Work?

Some of you may be thinking, "This feels forced. Will it work?" I trust that as you try these activities each day, you will see how important it is to

be intentional about creating the kind of relationship you want. My goal for you is to create a mindset where your relationship comes first. I hope to help you raise your awareness, learn important information, and gain skills that help sustain your relationship—and to experiment! Try everything once. If you love a tip, keep doing it. If you don't, tweak it! Highlight or bookmark the days you love the most and do them frequently. If you prefer different days than your partner, talk to each other about why those days appeal to you.

If there is a day that doesn't apply to you, use that day to connect with your partner in any way you'd like. Make it your day in a way that benefits your relationship. If the day calls for a physical act but your partner is out of town, use the next day's tip or reflection. If there's a tip about how to fight more effectively but you and your partner haven't fought recently, still take note of the tip and how you can practice it. You may need to swap some days and/or revisit others. Also, some tips are repeated because they're important to revisit.

ANITA A. CHLIPALA, LMFT

Areas of Focus

You may be wondering, "Why did you pick the tips that you did?" The couples that I work with come to me with the same problems. The information that I give and the skills that I teach my couples are found in this book, and they work—when practiced. The areas I want you to focus on for this next year are the ones that are critical to making your relationship the best it can be!

Friendship

Friendship is the foundation of a happy relationship. The more you know about each other, the stronger your relationship will be. My clients often tell me that focusing on their friendship makes the tough times a lot easier to handle.

Don't assume that you know everything about your partner. People change and grow; assuming you know everything closes you off from an opportunity to deepen your friendship. Be curry.

The tips will spark conversation—you will answer questions that will help you continue to know and learn about important similarities and differences. The more knowledge you have about your partner the better, and you will be more compassionate and understanding during conflicts.

Positivity

Having positivity is critical to the stability of a relationship. It is so easy to get overwhelmed with negativity. I will give you tips and skills to monitor and curb your negativity, but decreasing the negative is not enough—the positive must be intentionally created.

Love

It's common for people to give love in the way they want to receive it. Problems can arise because not everyone loves the same way with the same words and actions. Couples can feel unloved, uncared for, and disconnected from one another. Before you begin this book, I recommend that you take *The 5 Love Languages* quiz by Dr. Gary Chapman. Your top two love

ANITA A. CHLIPALA, LMFT

8

languages are your preferred way of giving and receiving love. Compare your languages to your partner's—are they similar or different? You will experience all five love languages throughout this next year while using this book. Be sure to discuss which love acts you liked and appreciated the most.

Communication & Conflict Resolution

Almost two-thirds of the time, couples won't see eye-to-eye on issues. It is more important to manage problems rather than solve them. It's also critical to accept what you can't change about your partner while negotiating what's most important to you. The tips in this book are geared to give you the skills and tools to manage the conflicts in ways that prevent them from weakening your relationship.

Emotional Management

In order to have constructive conversations, especially when attempting to solve problems, it's important to keep your cool. Expressing your thoughts,

behaviors, and emotions must be done carefully and with thoughtful consideration. Expressing negative emotions whenever you want and however you want can lead to an escalation of conflict, which greatly deteriorates relationships.

When you're in fight-or-flight mode, it's difficult to hear your partner, so you can throw understanding out the window. When you "lose it," this is also the time when you're more likely to say things you don't mean, dig in your heels, intentionally hurt your partner, bring up unrelated past conflicts, etc. If you are in "flight," you shut down and can also shut your partner out. It's OK to feel what you feel, but be responsible with your emotions. These tips will help you manage and express your emotions in healthy ways.

Fidelity

Most people think they will never cheat and assume their partner won't cheat either. They also assume the same definition of cheating and assume monogamy without talking about it. I work with a lot of couples strug-

gling with affairs, and none of my clients had any in-depth discussions about cheating prior to the infidelity. The tips included in this book are designed to open communication between you and your partner as well as take important steps to cheat-proof your relationship.

Novelty

One aspect of intimacy that my clients complain about is lack of passion. They definitely had passion in the beginning of their relationship, but that's also when everything was new. You had new experiences or even saw your world differently just because you had your partner by your side.

Whatever you call it—lust, infatuation, romantic love—it lasts, on average, for about 18 months. Once routine, comfort, and familiarity set in, passion can decrease. Couples can work on sustaining passion through variety and trying new things together.

Self

You're important. Some days will require you to focus on yourself—mak-

ing you a better person, taking inventory of yourself, doing things that you enjoy, and nurturing your own identity. Try not to put yourself last on your to-do list. You take care of your relationship by taking care of yourself.

Quotes

Quotes are provided to use as you wish. You can reflect on them on your own or share your reflections with your partner.

Final Thoughts

This book is not a "quick fix." It is about helping you build and maintain a healthy relationship. It is about increasing awareness of your own accountability, focusing on positives in your partner, using skills proven to help with communication and understanding, and doing the things to keep the love and passion burning.

Start today. Do not wait. Too many couples fall into the, "When this

ANITA A. CHLIPALA, LMFT

work deadline is over, when the kids go back to school, after the holidays, once my business really takes off, etc." trap. It is precisely during these busy times when you need each other the most. Sometimes you may have to swap a day for a different one more suited to your schedules. I get that; just try not to do it too often. The challenge for this next year is to do one thing every day. This book is purposefully not a calendar book. I do not want you to fall into the trap of "I'll start on January 1st." Start now.

A great relationship isn't something you just have or find, but something you achieve by focusing on and taking action. In a world that moves at lightning speed, where there is too much to do and too little time, I believe in, and want for you, lasting love. So cheers to a fabulous year, where this little book can help you create a relationship that blossoms each day when, "First comes us."

Day 1:

Recall 3 extremely happy and meaningful moments in your relationship. Share these with your partner.

Day 2:

Your relationship greatly benefits from quality time together. Define "quality time" and share your definitions. Provide concrete examples of your top 3 favorite ways of spending quality time with each other such as date night, weekend breakfast in bed, doing an activity together, etc.

Day 3:

Before you start your workday, know one thing that your partner will do today and ask them about it. Do they look forward to it? Does it stress them out?

Day 4:

Hug your partner at least 3 times today. Make 'em count!

Day 5:

Talk about it: What is your favorite way to spend an evening at home?

Day 6:

What activities do you find particularly exciting and exhilarating? Make a list and pick one to do together within the next month. (Save this list for future use in this book.)

———— ⋄∘☙❧∘⋄ ————

Day 7:

Create a ritual for the first 5–10 minutes of seeing each other after several hours' absence. For example, share a hug and kiss, and for 5 minutes one partner shares about their day. For the second 5 minutes, it's the other partner's turn.

Day 8:

Say this to your partner: "There's no one like you when it comes to
S_____."

Almost no one is foolish enough to imagine that he automatically deserves great success in any field of activity; yet almost everyone believes that he automatically deserves success in [relationships].

— SYDNEY J. HARRIS

———◇○〜○◇———

Day 9:

Make a list of 5–10 things you can do to self-soothe (what relaxes you and calms you down). For example, spend time with your pet, read a book, do yoga, meditate, etc. Make this list your go-to when you are stressed, worried, upset, or angry.

Day 10:

Be understood. Understanding only happens when your partner feels understood. You can check for understanding by rephrasing what you heard—"So I'm hearing that you're frustrated because…"—and asking questions such as, "Did I get that right?"

Day 11:

Talk about it: How was anger expressed in your family when you were growing up? How has that influenced the way you are comfortable with expressing anger in your present relationship?

Day 12:

What makes you happy? Spend a few minutes today and write down all of the things, people, experiences, etc., that make you happy and fulfilled. Look over this list and circle the items that you have neglected. Discuss your list with your partner, and pick one item to do for yourself within the week.

Day 13:

Appreciation is so important in relationships. Tell your partner why you appreciate them. Pick at least 3 traits or behaviors and be specific. Say and/or show gratitude for their awesomeness. You can text, leave a note, or share in person.

Day 14:

Make a list of all the things that you both loved about your time when you were dating. Circle at least 3 items that you both would like to do in the next month and put them on the calendar.

ANITA A. CHLIPALA, LMFT

Day 15:

Playfully slap or grab your partner's butt when they pass by you.

Day 16:

Cheating can happen in 3 ways: emotionally, sexually, and a combination of the two. People often assume monogamy without clearly defining what it is. What do you both consider to be cheating? Discuss concrete examples.

Day 17:

Write a love note with an actual pen and paper. Use a sticky note, a card, exchange a journal—get creative! Mail it or leave it in a place your partner will find.

Day 18:

Talk about it: What does money mean to you? How is it important to you? How was money treated in your family when you were young? How does that influence the way you presently handle money?

Day 19:

Contempt is a predictor of divorce. Forms of contempt include: rolling your eyes, name-calling, hostile humor, mockery, and sarcasm. Pay attention to when you use these behaviors toward your partner and eliminate them.

Love is saying, "I feel differently" instead of "You're wrong."

— ANONYMOUS

Day 20:

Pay attention to your partner's interests. What gifts reflect these interests? Get a gift for your partner within the week. If finances are a concern, think of low-budget gifts that still show you pay attention to details about your partner's likes.

Day 21:

Define "respect." What does it look like and mean to both of you? Share concrete examples of how your partner can show respect toward you.

Day 22:

When you're watching TV, make out during commercial breaks.

Day 23:

Can you name your partner's 3 current stressors? If yes, ask if you can support him or her in any way. If not, find out today what is giving them stress and how you can support them.

Day 24:

Inside jokes strengthen connections. What inside jokes do you already share? Use them frequently and don't forget to create more!

Day 25:

How do you transition from "work mode" to "home mode"? If you don't, create a ritual. Do you need 15 minutes of alone time? A shower? A 5-minute shoulder rub?

Day 26:

Talk about it: What are your favorite childhood memories? Which memories would you rather forget? What could have made your bad memories better? How have these influenced who you are today and what you want and need in your relationship?

Day 27:

Ask your partner: "What can I help you with today?"

Day 28:

When you get upset, do you get heated or do you shut down? The goal is to call a time-out before you get to that point, and then regroup to talk about what happened when you're feeling calmer. The person who calls the time-out should initiate the time-in.

Whenever you're in conflict with someone, there is one factor that can make the difference between damaging your relationship and deepening it. That factor is attitude.

— WILLIAM JAMES

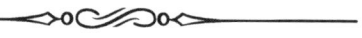

Day 29:

What drives your partner crazy (in a good way)? Do this.

Day 30:

Talk about it: Which of your efforts would you like your partner to recognize more often?

Day 31:

Sometimes conversations turn into disagreements because of bad timing. If you're preoccupied and can't give 100% of your attention to your partner, if you're in a bad mood, if you want to relax, etc., let them know! You can say something like, "Can we talk about this later?" Be sure to carve out time for a discussion when the timing is better.

Day 32:

Get your needs met. Write down a list of your 5–10 core needs—physical affection, fun, security, loyalty, conversation, etc. Are these being met? Which ones can your partner help meet? So they understand what your expectations are, describe these needs to your partner—what does fun look like? Is a 15-minute a day conversation enough to meet your need for conversation? Be specific. It is not realistic for your partner to fulfill all of your needs all of the time, so think of which needs you can sometimes fulfill on your own.

Day 33:

If it's a struggle to not talk about work or children during date night, do some prep beforehand. Share interesting articles that you recently read; brush up on sports and current events; ask about family or friends, dreams, or goals; or talk about the future.

Day 34:

Cuddle without the expectation of sex. (But if it leads to sex, that's OK, too!)

Day 35:

Tell your partner: "You brighten my day when you _____."

Day 36:

Create a morning ritual with your partner. For example: kiss and hug good-bye, say "I love you," and share one thing each of you will do that day.

Day 37:

Buy a gift card to your partner's favorite store. Give it to them creatively (taped to their favorite candy, with a loving note, leaving it on their pillow, etc.).

Day 38:

Talk about it: Do you think you have a purpose in life? When you leave this world, how will you have wanted to make an impact?

What counts in making a happy [relationship] is not so much how compatible you are, but how you deal with incompatibility.

— LEO TOLSTOY

Day 39:

What is "good sex"? Share your thoughts with your partner.

Day 40:

Monitor the negative assumptions you are making about your partner. Do you automatically believe these assumptions or do you check out their accuracy with your partner? Challenge yourself to think of your partner's positive intentions, and if you're still in doubt, check it out with your partner.

Day 41:

Talk about it: What makes you feel competent? What makes you feel insecure?

Day 42:

Some people need more time to calm down or process a fight. How much time do you usually need after a disagreement or fight? Share this with your partner and respect what they need, too.

Day 43:

Define "closeness." What does it look like? What specific things make you feel closest to your partner? Clarify: "When you initiate love-making" vs. "Sex." "When we talk about things other than work and kids" vs. "Conversation." Think of at least 2–3 things to share.

Day 44:

Give your partner a hot/sexy compliment at an inopportune time—such as right before walking into a restaurant for brunch with friends.

Day 45:

Make a list of your most important values. Try to keep the list to 5–10. Share with your partner why these are so important to you.

Day 46:

Talk about it: What are your partner's short- and long-term personal goals? How can you support making these goals a reality?

No partner in a love relationship ... should feel that he has to give up an essential part of himself to make it viable.

— MAY SARTON

Day 47:

Discuss any fears about being cheated on by your partner.

Day 48:

Make it a rule to not call, text, or email when you're very upset or angry. Communicating in this emotional state is not a good idea because you risk sending messages that are hurtful and that you don't mean.

Day 49:

Have a 10–20-minute gripe session where you complain about what's bothering you, stressing you out, worrying you, etc. An important rule: you don't talk about your relationship during these sessions.

Day 50:

Talk about it: What is your favorite and least favorite holiday? Why?

ANITA A. CHLIPALA, LMFT

Day 51:

What are nonphysical ways to have foreplay that you really enjoy? Add your partner's preferences into lovemaking this week.

Day 52:

Ask yourself: "Would I want to live with me?" Do you like your answer? Identify 2–3 areas that you can improve on (e.g., not nagging, being more patient, being more present to your partner, etc.).

Day 53:

Ask your partner: "When did you feel most loved by me?"

In a good relationship, people get angry, but in a very different way. The [Relationship] Masters see a problem a bit like a soccer ball. They kick it around. It's "our" problem.

— John Gottman

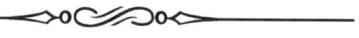

Day 54:

What outfit of your partner's is your favorite? Why? Share this with them. Both of you can wear these outfits on your next date or when appropriate.

Day 55:

Own your experiences, feelings, and thoughts by using "I" statements during conversations and disagreements. For example, "I'd like to spend more time with you" vs. "You're ignoring me." You're much more likely to get what you want. The added perk: "I" statements reduce defensiveness in your partner.

Day 56:

Have you been putting off a request by your partner? Make the time to make it happen within the week.

Day 57:

What are 5 qualities that you adore about your partner? Tell them.

Day 58:

Just because you don't see things the same way doesn't mean that you're not right for each other. No matter whom you're with, you will never see eye-to-eye on all issues. Respecting your differences and not allowing them to engulf you both in negativity is key to relationship success. How can you celebrate and accept your differences? How does your life and relationship benefit from the differences your partner has?

Day 59:

How do you communicate, verbally and nonverbally, that you are sorry? Does your partner view these actions and words as remorse? Share with each other.

Day 60:

Talk about it: What does "fun and playfulness" look like for you both?

Love is the only thing you get more of by giving it away.

— Tom Wilson

Day 61:

A key ingredient to a happy sex life is the ability to talk about sex. Without becoming reactive (watch so you don't take things personally), what does sex mean to you? How important is it? When do you feel the most connected to each other? What can make your sex life better?

Day 62:

Slow dance with your partner.

Day 63:

Define "love." How do you know that your partner truly loves and cares for you? How are your definitions (and thus expectations) different?

Day 64:

Based on the discussion from Day 63, give love to your partner in the way they want to receive it.

Day 65:

When you want to blame your partner, think, "Where am I accountable for what happened? Could I have done something differently? Better?"

Day 66:

Tell your partner: "What I have learned from you is _____."

Day 67:

How do you show your partner that you desire them sexually? What would they like you to do more often? Share with each other.

Day 68:

Schedule a meeting once or twice a week to discuss expectations around weekly responsibilities: chores, errands, family events, financial obligations, appointments, etc. Decide on a day and time. Create a brief agenda to keep you on track.

Day 69:

Shower together.

Day 70:

Do you complain to others about your partner? This opens the door for an emotional bond with others where they can align with you and put down your partner. Instead, do your best to resolve your conflicts directly with your partner.

ANITA A. CHLIPALA, LMFT

Day 71:

Talk about it: What are 2–3 things that make you angry that have nothing to do with your partner?

Day 72:

Do you and your partner still flirt with each other? If yes, what do you like the most? If not, what do you miss? Keep your relationship light and playful with frequent flirting.

To dream the person you would like your partner to be is to waste the person your partner is.

— ANONYMOUS

Day 73:

What is your favorite way that your partner touches you? Tell them.

Day 74:

Text your partner: "Tonight I will _____."

Day 75:

What is your partner's favorite candy, beverage, etc.? Buy it for them soon.

Day 76:

Nobody likes to be criticized. It's OK to be upset with something that your partner said or did, but criticizing your partner won't bring about what you want. Instead, frame it as a request: What is it that you want? What do you desire and need? Keep the tone positive. For example, say, "I would like you to help out more like you said you would," instead of, "You're so lazy."

Day 77:

Ask your partner: "What is one thing I can do to make your life better?"

Day 78:

What are 3–5 strategies that help get you out of a funk?

Day 79:

How do you make your partner feel wanted like nobody else in this world?

Day 80:

Say this to your partner: "I appreciate when you say/do _____ because it makes me feel _____."

Day 81:

Use "pause" and "replay" frequently. If your conversation isn't going the way you would like it to go, call a "pause" to stop the conversation and go back to a point where you can start over.

Day 82:

Talk about it: Out of all the people that you dated, why did you decide to get into a long-term relationship with/marry your partner?

Day 83:

What's your favorite behavior or activity that reenergizes you when you are stressed out or exhausted? Make time for it soon.

The most important [relationship] skill is listening to your partner in a way that they can't possibly doubt that you love them.

— DIANE SOLLEE

Day 84:

How do you know you can trust your partner? What are they doing that shows you they are trustworthy? Share your thoughts with each other. Brainstorm other ways you can increase trust.

Day 85:

What's your game plan for life's stresses? How do you act like a team and face stressors together? Create a list of things you can both do that help buffer your relationship from stress.

Day 86:

Create a making-up ritual. After conflict, how would you both like to reconnect?

Day 87:

Do you take things personally? When your partner does or says something and your first instinct is to take it personally, take a few moments to think of other possibilities that have nothing to do with you.

Day 88:

What are the fundamental differences between you and your partner? Showing up late vs. being on time? Spontaneous vs. planner? Keeping the peace vs. liking a good debate? How can you show acceptance of these differences? For example, challenge yourself to see the positives and values in what your partner wants or believes.

Day 89:

Plan another activity from your Day 6 list.

Day 90:

Plan a meal, shop for the necessary groceries, and cook it together within a week.

The way to change others' minds is with affection, and not anger.

— DALAI LAMA

Day 91:

Talk about it: When you were sick as a child, what did you find most comforting?

Day 92:

You can't tell someone what to do, but you can stop negativity or unwanted behavior from coming at you by establishing boundaries. Identify and discuss what behaviors you don't want directed at you, such as name-calling, yelling, being treated like a child, etc.

Day 93:

You can reinforce boundaries with a word or a phrase such as, "Please stop," "I need a time-out," or "Let's take a break."

Day 94:

Wwhat are your partner's personality quirks? How can you demon-strate acceptance of these quirks? How did you show acceptance when you were dating?

Day 95:

Do you know which chore your partner despises the most? Do it for them this week.

Day 96:

If you're married, make it a rule to never use the word "divorce" during a fight. If you're in a long-term relationship, make it a rule to not threaten to break up. This behavior erodes trust and a sense of security.

Day 97:

How involved are your extended families in your relationship/family? Is this working for your relationship or not? If not, discuss what you would both like to see. At a minimum, establish basic ground rules and expectations of your relatives toward your partner and relationship. For example, your partner is invited to all family events or you alternate holiday dinners.

Day 98:

Go on a double-date with friends soon.

Day 99:

Talk about it: Are birthdays important to you or "just another day"? How would you feel if your partner forgot your birthday? What are ways that your partner can make your birthday meaningful and special if it's important to you?

first *comes* **US:** The Busy Couple's Guide *to lasting love*

Married couples who love each other tell each other a thousand things without talking.

— CHINESE PROVERB

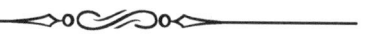

Day 100:

Negative interactions can pack a bigger punch than positive ones. Make an extra effort to notice all of the positive things your partner is doing today or has recently done.

Day 101:

Manage your anxiety. Do you recognize when you have anxiety? When you're anxious, what thoughts do you have? Where do you feel it in your body? Sometimes people look to their partner to help manage their anxiety, but being a self-responsible partner also means managing it on your own. Use your strategies to self-soothe and question the validity of your thoughts: Are you assuming the worst? Taking it personally? Magnifying a problem?

Day 102:

Tell your partner: "If you were not in my life, I would miss _____."

Day 103:

Cards never go out of style. Buy your partner a card, but don't forget to add a special, personalized note.

Day 104:

Transparency is key to increasing trust in your relationship. How do you show your partner that you have nothing to hide?

Day 105:

What do you like for sexual afterplay?

—◦◦◦◦—

Day 106:

Whether on the phone or in person, brag about your partner to other people. Bonus points if your partner is present to witness it.

Day 107:

What fun activity have the both of you been putting off? Make a plan to do this activity together soon.

Day 108:

Create a weekend morning ritual. For example: breakfast in bed; or coffee, morning paper, and conversation, etc.

Love requires respect and friendship as well as passion. Because there comes a time when you have to get out of bed.

— ERICA JONG

⟨∘C∽⟩∘⟨

Day 109:

Talk about it: What are your short-term and long-term financial goals? What are your worries, if any, about financial hardships?

Day 110:

Share with your partner 2 ways you appreciate "Me Time." This is time when you get to be alone to recharge. Make "Me Time" happen this week.

Day 111:

Say this to your partner: "One thing I wish you knew about me is S_____."

Day 112:

Here's a mantra for your relationship: Reinforce the behaviors that you want to keep. Acknowledge at least 3 of your partner's actions that you appreciate and want to continue. Don't just say, "Thank you" or "I liked that." Say, "Thank you, that meant a lot to me because…" or "I liked that because it showed me that you…"

Day 113:

When you're in the middle of an argument and your partner asks to stop the conversation, respect their need for space. Revisit the discussion when your partner is ready.

Day 114:

How do you support your partner with their family, friends, coworkers, and bosses? Even if you disagree with your partner or want to play mediator, it's important to show your partner that you align with him or her.

Day 115:

During disagreements, stick with the issue at hand. Bringing up past hurts/unresolved topics can do more harm than good.

Day 116:

Define "romance." Be as concrete and detailed as possible. Do an activity within the next few days that is based on your partner's definition of romance.

When you make a sacrifice in [a relationship], you're sacrificing not to each other but to unity in a relationship.

— JOSEPH CAMPBELL

Day 117:

The more you have sex, the more you're going to want it. So just do it already!

Day 118:

When having a conversation about a hot topic, keep your statements brief. It's much easier to understand your points if there's a dialogue and not a monologue.

Day 119:

Talk about it: What are your views about freedom and independence? Are these important to you? Why or why not?

Day 120:

Listening to your partner is a solution. You do not have to problem-solve each time. Demonstrate understanding before you provide advice or solutions. You can also ask your partner, "What do you need from me right now?"

Day 121:

Create a bedtime ritual: pillow talk, cuddling, rubbing noses, etc.

Day 122:

To remain connected and show respect, it is more important to show understanding of your partner's perspective than it is to solve every problem you and your partner have. You can start by saying something like, "I get your point," or "That part makes sense."

Day 123:

Talk about it: Do you like to be surprised? What kind of surprises do you like? Within the next couple of weeks, surprise your partner with what they like.

Being heard is so close to being loved that for the average person, they are almost indistinguishable.

— DAVID AUGSBURGER

Day 124:

Share what "little things" about your partner you enjoy the most.

Day 125:

Does your partner tell you that they feel like they can't do anything right? Your partner will never do things the exact same way that you would, so let the little things slide. Show your partner appreciation for the things they do take care of.

Day 126:

Ever have those arguments about what was said in the past? Memories are faulty, so it's pointless to persist in what was actually said or done, and those arguments end up going nowhere. An alternate approach is to shift to the present, and say something like, "Let me please tell you what I meant to say."

Day 127:

Self-disclosure builds trust and intimacy. Is there anything that gets in the way of self-disclosure (e.g., your partner's reaction to unpleasant news or a past bad relationship)? What are 1–2 things that can help you be more open with your partner?

Day 128:

This week, make love somewhere other than your bed or typical spot.

Day 129:

Practice a mantra so that you can be prepared before you "lose it" or shut down in a disagreement. Something like, "I need to calm down" can help prevent a disagreement from escalating out of control.

Day 130:

Talk about it: What's one thing you want to do or accomplish within the next 10 years?

The life and love we create is the life and love we live.

— LEO BUSCAGLIA

Day 131:

Be as detailed as you can with what you're looking for from your partner. Instead of saying, "I need you to be more loving," say, "I need you to do _____ because then I feel loved."

Day 132:

If you're in a crabby mood, how can you let your partner know (in a nice way, of course) so they don't inadvertently make things worse?

Day 133:

Body-map each other. Take two pieces of paper and each of you draw a figure. No peeking! Mark the areas on the body where you think your partner likes to be touched. Now compare notes.

Day 134:

Humor reduces stress and stimulates the brain areas associated with pleasure and reward. Joke around with each other and make your partner laugh!

Day 135:

Going to bed angry is better than marathon conversations that wear you both out and can potentially make things worse. Take a break from the issue and try again when you are rested.

Day 136:

Make out for at least 15 minutes—but leave on all of your clothes!

Day 137:

Talk about it: How did your family resolve conflicts when you were growing up? How has that influenced the way you resolve conflicts with your partner?

Day 138:

Say this to your partner: "I find it incredibly hot when you S_____."

Day 139:

What are your dreams? What are your partner's dreams? Although your initial reaction may be "No" or "That's not possible," how can you both support each other in achieving your dreams?

———— ⟩०〇⟨〇⟩०〇⟨ ————

A friend is someone whose face lights up when they see you ... and who doesn't have any immediate plans for your improvement.

— BILL COFFIN

first *comes* **US:** The Busy Couple's Guide *to lasting love*

Day 140:

It can be expensive to go out. If money is a concern, brainstorm as many activities as you can that are on a budget. Improv or comedy shows, free museum days, wine or beer tastings, street festivals, going out for ice cream and walking around the city, BYOB restaurants, the zoo, and free concerts in the park are just some ideas to get you started.

Day 141:

Tit-for-tat is extremely destructive. No matter how badly your partner acts, don't use it as a reason to also behave badly. Accountability to your relationship is to still act responsibly and respectfully. Call a time-out if necessary to avoid escalation of conflict.

Day 142:

Create a ritual to transition from the daily grind to getting into the mood.

Day 143:

Ask your partner: "When was the last time you did something out of your comfort zone?"

Day 144:

Write a sticky note with an affirming/sexy message, and leave it in a place where only your partner will find it.

Day 145:

Share your high/low of the day.

Day 146:

Stay in and order food to be delivered. Challenge: Make love before the food gets to your door.

Day 147:

U se phrases such as, "Looking forward to tonight…" and "Can't wait to see you…"

Love is the irresistible desire to be irresistibly desired.

— ROBERT FROST

Day 148:

Have a Potential Threat Check: coworkers, neighbors, your favorite barista at your local coffee joint, acquaintances, etc. Any concerns about these people? What are your rules and boundaries regarding these people? What concrete steps do you both have to take to enforce these boundaries? For example, you both will not do or say anything that you would not be comfortable doing in front of your partner.

Day 149:

Talk about it: What significant events are coming up in your partner's life? How do they feel about them? Be sure to empathize with their feelings (i.e., "I can see why you would feel…")

Day 150:

Your partner lets you know what they like. How do they spend their free time? What do they like to do to relax? What excites them? What do they look forward to? Turn one of these into a tangible gift.

Day 151:

When was your partner reliable? Tell them.

Day 152:

Negative emotions are not bad; they provide you with information. What is critical is to be able to safely talk about and understand negative emotions, events, and interactions with each other. Discuss ways that you can increase safety in your relationship. For example, "If I say I can't talk about this right now, please respect that."

Day 153:

Say this to your partner: "When I am in a bad mood I need S_____."

Day 154:

Volunteer together.

Day 155:

Hug for at least 60 seconds.

A kiss is a lovely trick designed by nature to stop speech when words become superfluous.

— INGRID BERGMAN

Day 156:

Reasoning with your partner's emotions won't work (such as saying, "Don't feel that way."). It's another way of minimizing what they are feeling. Instead, show empathy and compassion by repeating back what you're hearing, asking more questions, saying, "I can understand why that must be _____ for you..."

Day 157:

How does your partner try to get your attention? Do you think you are giving them the attention they desire? What do they say? If there's a discrepancy, identify 1–2 ways you can give your partner the attention they want.

Day 158:

Talk about it: If you could have any talent, what would it be?

Day 159:

Ask yourself, "Do I make it easy for others to live with me?" And this isn't limited to physical space, but also your interactions, reactions, etc. Do you like your answer? Pick one thing that you can improve to make it easier to live with you.

Day 160:

Give a small gift that lets your partner know they are on your mind.

Day 161:

One night this week, at least one hour before bedtime, turn off all electronics and spend quality time together.

Day 162:

Sometimes people have different ways they sexually express themselves. Create a "Yes, No, Maybe" list to brainstorm things you would do, would never do, and are open to doing sexually.

Day 163:

What vacation would you want to take with your partner, just the two of you? Where would you go and what would you do together? If money and time were no object, what would be your ideal vacation? Share with each other.

Love doesn't just sit there like a stone; it has to be made, like bread, remade all the time, made new.

— URSULA K. LE GUIN

—◦❦◦—

ANITA A. CHLIPALA, LMFT

Day 164:

Get dressed up and go out.

Day 165:

Create a ritual to celebrate personal successes and achievements with your partner. For example, go out to your favorite restaurant or enjoy a bottle of champagne at home.

Day 166:

Talk about it: What actions and words do you find "disrespectful"? Increase your awareness of these behaviors and try to decrease or eliminate them.

Day 167:

Y ou should be each other's #1 fans. How do you support, encourage, and cheer on your partner? How does your partner want to receive your encouragement and praise? Do it more often.

Day 168:

I t's natural to want to defend yourself against your partner's negativity. You want to prove your good intentions to your partner. This is good in theory but not in practice. Defensiveness won't lead to positive change or closeness. Instead, tell your partner you need time to think about what they said. Take this time for reflection: What was your partner right about? What do you disagree with and why? When you are calm, discuss with your partner.

Day 169:

T alk about your fantasies, even if you'd never act on them.

ANITA A. CHLIPALA, LMFT

Day 170:

Say this to your partner: "You're an awesome partner/parent because
S_____."

Day 171:

Do something differently today: Go for a walk after dinner, surprise
your partner, explore a new area of your city or neighboring town,
etc.

Day 172:

Ask your partner: "What are your pet peeves?"

Day 173:

When did you know you loved your partner? Share this moment or
time with them.

———— ⤖⟡⤖ ————

The grass looks greener on the other side of the fence only because we don't have to mow it.

— SHIRLEY GLASS

Day 174:

Play a board or card game together.

Day 175:

Talk about it: What's on your partner's "Bucket List"?

Day 176:

Plan a mystery date. For example, email/text or leave a note on the fridge with the day, time, and address of your date. Only include the most pertinent information (e.g., recommended attire).

Day 177:

Schedule sex this week. Do what you need to do to get yourself in the mood by this day.

Day 178:

Create a surplus of positivity. Go out of your way to notice and point out the positives in your partner and your relationship.

Day 179:

Make these phrases part of your conversation when things get too heated during a disagreement:

Can we take a break?   Please listen to me.
Time out.   Let's agree to disagree.
Can we start over?   We're getting off track.
Let me rephrase that.   I'm sorry.

Day 180:

Your relationship should be like Vegas—what happens in your relationship, stays in your relationship. Complaining to your friends and family about your partner cracks the foundation of your relationship. The only person who knows why they acted the way that they did is your partner, so address the issues directly with them.

Day 181:

Share five 20-second hugs today.

Day 182:

Talk about it: What makes you jealous?

Commitment is making a choice to give up other choices.

— Scott Stanley

Day 183:

Do a relationship status check. Some questions to consider: What's going well in your relationship? What can be improved? Are you both happy? Are your needs getting met? How's your friendship? Is there enough appreciation in the relationship? Do you feel taken for granted?

Day 184:

Do you avoid conflict with your partner? What are your concerns? Check if you are assuming the worst or think disaster will strike if you tell your partner your thoughts and feelings.

Day 185:

Buy or make your partner's favorite dessert or snack.

Day 186:

Play hooky and make it a special day for you and partner.

Day 187:

Keep a running list of activities that you enjoy: Reading, running, golfing, fishing, going to concerts, socializing with friends, trying new cuisines, etc. Make one of these happen within a week. Never stop the things that bring you pleasure and make you you.

Day 188:

Are you helping to create an environment where your partner looks forward to coming home? What can be improved? Let your partner know one thing that would help, such as a kiss hello or waiting until after dinner to tackle the to-do list.

Day 189:

Plan a "Reverse Date"—have sex first and then go out on your date.

Day 190:

Get crafty! Make a coupon for your partner that they can redeem. It can be for a chore, for doing an activity with them, for a massage, etc.

Day 191:

Talk about it: What is your recipe for happiness?

[A relationship] is an investment which pays dividends if you pay interest.

— BOB MONKHOUSE

ANITA A. CHLIPALA, LMFT

Day 192:

Revisit your cheating definition. Are there any additions you would like to add?

Day 193:

Everyone has "buttons" that can be unintentionally pushed by a partner. What are yours? For example, feeling excluded, like a failure, rejected, inferior, abandoned, ignored, etc. Discuss with each other. Be gentle with each other's sensitivities.

Day 194:

Have a night out with your friends soon, either together or separately.

Day 195:

Reminisce about your first date. What do you remember? What was your favorite moment?

Day 196:

Take a bubble bath together.

Day 197:

Ask your partner: "What can I help you with right now?"

Day 198:

Learn to forgive yourself. Everyone goofs up now and again—it doesn't make you a bad person. What can you learn, or have you already learned, from your mistakes?

Day 199:

Appreciate the here-and-now instead of chasing after future satisfactions ("When I…" and "If only…"). Name 3 things that you appreciate today.

—————⋄∘〰∘⋄—————

Day 200:

Change it up: Schedule a date night on a night when you usually don't go out.

Day 201:

Notice if you've been criticizing or complaining about your partner lately. How can you state this criticism or complaint in a positive way? For example, instead of, "You never talk to me," try, "I'd like to know what goes on during your day. It would make me feel closer to you."

Be sure to taste your words before you spit them out.

— Unknown

Day 202:

Talk about it: If you could get away with the perfect crime, what would you do?

Day 203:

Describe to each other what you like about having sex. You both decide if you want it to be during the moment or a scheduled conversation (or both!).

Day 204:

Create a ritual around birthdays. Things to consider: Where do you celebrate the day? Is anyone with you or is it a moment for just the two of you? What do you want to do? Do you take the whole day off?

Day 205:

This week, when your partner does something that annoys/frustrates you, first give them the benefit of the doubt that it was not intentional. Second, think what the positive intention might have been behind their action. If you can let it go, great. If it still bothers you, bring it to their attention in a gentle way.

Day 206:

What are ways that you can help each other calm down? Discuss things that you like and that work for you.

Day 207:

When you're in a public area, whisper in your partner's ear, "If we were alone right now I'd _____."

Day 208:

Talk about it: What are you most proud of in your relationship? In your life, as a child and as an adult?

Day 209:

Laugh! Laughter not only feels good, but it brings couples closer to each other. Watch a funny movie or go to a comedy or improv show.

Day 210:

Have a gripe session. Spend 20 minutes each talking about what is currently causing you stress, anxiety, worry, etc. Keep it about things other than your relationship.

Day 211:

Plan a weekend brunch together.

Day 212:

Pick one area where you would like your partner to demonstrate more support (e.g., taking the children to their lessons, visiting sick relatives, chores around the house). Make your partner's request happen soon.

Day 213:

Talk about it: What do you dislike most about yourself? (For the listener, try to empathize and be supportive and not minimize your partner's perception of themselves.)

Come to the edge, A said.
I'm afraid, B said.
Come to the edge, A said.
I'm afraid, B said.
Come to the edge, A said.
And B came to the edge.
Jump, A said.
And B jumped.
And B flew.

— ANONYMOUS

Day 214:

Have sex this week. Take the time to find a new position that you haven't done yet but are both willing to try.

Day 215:

Plan a picnic—have it at the office, outside, or at home. Plan the meal together.

Day 216:

Talk about it: What event(s) has been the most instrumental in shaping your life?

Day 217:

Be playfully competitive with each other. Play a video game, go mini golfing, or do another activity that you both enjoy.

Day 218:

On a dinner date, make it a challenge to keep the talk about work and children before the drinks or appetizers come. After the drinks and appetizers, it's a "No Work and Kids Zone."

Day 219:

Make your partner's favorite meal within the week. Take a little time today to plan it.

Day 220:

Stop, Drop, and Kiss!

Love thrives on trivial kindnesses.

— THEODOR FONTANE

Day 221:

Happy couples are extremely kind to one another. Make an extra effort to show kindness today.

Day 222:

Toasts don't have to be reserved for special occasions. Make a toast on your next date night.

Day 223:

Besides "Because I love him/her," why are you with your partner? Share these reasons with each other.

Day 224:

When your partner brings up something that is bothering them or they are unhappy with, try not to minimize it by brushing it off, telling them that it's "not a big deal," saying they should "just get over it," etc. In essence, the message you're giving your partner is that their feelings/experiences don't matter. Instead, ask questions—understand their point of view and why they feel/think like they do. The point is not to agree—the point is to understand.

Day 225:

When are the moments that you find your partner most attractive? When they are dressed up? Engaging in a hobby? Goofing off with your children? Tell them.

Lust is easy. Love is hard. Like is most important.

— CARL REINER

Day 226:

Talk about it: What are your rules and boundaries about contact with exes?

Day 227:

How do you convey that what your partner is feeling is important and valid? If you struggle in this area, ask your partner how you can show understanding. For example, you might say, "That sucks, babe," or "That is frustrating."

Day 228:

Revisit your financial goals. Are you on track? Are your values about money both being honored?

Day 229:

Have a night to yourself where you do something that relaxes or energizes you.

Day 230:

Y ou don't try to change your friends, you accept them for who they are. Do you apply this same attitude to your partner or do you try to change them? What do they say when you do? Apply to your partner the things you practice to be able to accept your friends.

Day 231:

T alk about it: What turns you off sexually?

Day 232:

P ut in the effort to look your best for your partner today.

Day 233:

S educe your partner this week.

Day 234:

The day after making love, relive it by talking about it. What was your favorite part? What would you like more of?

Day 235:

Do you maintain standards that are difficult to live up to? Do you expect your partner to live up to these standards, too? What do they say on this topic?

Day 236:

Your partner is not your clone. Catch yourself when you use words like "should" and "ought," especially when you are directing them toward your partner. Respect that they may have their own way of doing things.

Day 237:

Are you creating an environment where your partner can be vulnerable with you? Even if you don't immediately understand why they are feeling what they are feeling, asking questions and supporting them in their feelings will allow your partner to be more open with you.

Day 238:

Talk about it: What was the most difficult time in your life? How did you overcome it?

Love is not blind, it sees but it doesn't mind.

— RIZI JANE BALDON

Day 239:

Give your partner a massage. Use oils and candles to heighten the senses.

Day 240:

Taking care of yourself = stress management. You owe it to your relationship to take care of yourself, too. Make time for you today.

Day 241:

How did your partner meet their best friend? Why is this person their best friend?

Day 242:

When you have anxiety about your partner not doing something the "right" way, ask yourself, "What's the benefit of doing it their way?" What can you accept and let go? If you struggle, have a conversation with your partner about your difficulties.

Day 243:

Talk about it: What is your favorite location to make out? Visit this spot soon.

Day 244:

Develop a common interest together. Take a class or training, or pick an activity you both would like to try.

Day 245:

Missing each other is a good thing. Do one or both of you need some alone time? When do you need space away from your partner?

Day 246:

Conflict resolution is not about one person having to change or give up something that is important to them. How can you accommodate both of your needs and desires through compromise? Brainstorm multiple solutions, and experiment with which ones work for both of you. Remember, compromise will never feel perfect.

Day 247:

For one week, sleep naked—both of you.

Day 248:

Catch yourself when you use the words "always" and "never" about your partner.

Day 249:

When your partner is speaking, don't give advice until asked. You can also ask, "How can I be of help right now?"

Day 250:

Talk about it: Do you prefer silly or romantic? Does the environment of your relationship reflect your preference? How can you both nurture the silly and/or romantic? Be specific.

Day 251:

Does your relationship have a guideline to decrease the probability of cheating? For example, "If I can't do this in front of my partner, I shouldn't be doing it." Discuss guidelines to protect your relationship.

Assumptions are the termites of relationships.

— HENRY WINKLER

———⇔o〰o⇔———

Day 252:

Say this to your partner: "I find you irresistible when you
S_____."

Day 253:

When you're in another room and your partner is cooking a meal, go
to your partner and passionately kiss them in the kitchen!

Day 254:

Take out your list from Day 6 and schedule another activity.

Day 255:

Find 5 things that your partner said/did in the last 24 hours that you
enjoyed and appreciated. Tell them.

Day 256:

It's easier to hear your partner when you aren't busy planning your own response. Put aside your own agenda to focus on your partner's experiences. Be sure to rephrase what you heard to ensure understanding.

We tend to judge others by their behavior, and ourselves by our intentions.

— ALBERT F. SCHLIEDER

ANITA A. CHLIPALA, LMFT

Day 257:

Talk about it: What is your favorite decade? What fad did you like the most? The least?

Day 258:

Do you confide in people besides your partner? You risk creating an emotional bond with others and undermining your relationship. Keep important issues between you and your partner.

Day 259:

Has something been bothering you but you haven't shared it with your partner? Are you bottling something up? Calmly and gently let your partner know what is bothering you. Use "I" statements and keep to one issue at a time.

Day 260:

Have a quickie! No excuses. Don't think about it, just do it!

Day 261:

Talk about it: What are your fears and doubts?

Day 262:

Even though you both know you love and care for each other, verbally remind each other of just how much you both mean to each other.

Day 263:

What do you remember about your first kiss?

Day 264:

Make a regular meal special. Light some candles, play music in the background, dress up, etc.

Love me when I least deserve it, because that's when I really need it.

— SWEDISH PROVERB

Day 265:

Revisit a special place from when you were dating—where you first met, your first date, place of engagement, etc. If that is not possible due to relocation, get creative! Go to the restaurant you first went to in your new town, the place of your favorite memory in your new location, etc.

Day 266:

Hug...naked.

Day 267:

In an argument, do you bring up previous screwups and past faults? Make it a ground rule to focus on the current issue. This will help you build safety in your communication.

Day 268:

Take a picture together and make it the wallpaper of your phone.

Day 269:

How do you celebrate your anniversary? Create a ritual for this day to connect in an extra special way.

Day 270:

When you're in the car together, put your hand on your partner's thigh.

Day 271:

Love competition? Outdo your partner with acts of love and admiration this week.

Day 272:

Don't withhold sex as punishment. Address the real issues.

Day 273:

Talk about it: What was your scariest moment when you were a child? As an adult?

True love stories never have endings.

— RICHARD BACH

Day 274:

Although some traits remain stable, people also change over time. Since you first met, how have you both changed? In your attitudes, beliefs, etc.? How do you continue to change? How can you mutually support these changes?

Day 275:

Talk about it: What are your spiritual/religious beliefs, if any? Is your faith where you want it to be? What role did religion/spirituality play in your childhood?

Day 276:

We make mistakes, and when we accept responsibility, we correct them. How does your partner try to correct their mistakes? Do they make your favorite meal? Say, "I'm sorry"? Pay attention to these attempts to mend any damage and acknowledge their efforts.

Day 277:

Go for a walk together.

Day 278:

What do you complain about the most? What is the actual want or need? You are more likely to get what you want if you turn that complaint into a request.

Day 279:

Plan a mini-vacation, even if it's only for a day or a weekend getaway.

Day 280:

Take a trip down memory lane: How did you two meet? Reminisce.

Day 281:

Alternate responsibility for date night this month.

Day 282:

Talk about it: Is there something that you've dreamed of doing but haven't yet? What's prevented you from doing this?

I love you the more in that I believe you had liked me for my own sake and for nothing else.

— JOHN KEATS

first *comes* **US:** The Busy Couple's Guide *to lasting love*

Day 283:

What errand(s) can you help your partner with this week?

Day 284:

Dealing with negative emotions doesn't have to be stressful—it just may take extra effort. Offer patience, compassion, and understanding.

Day 285:

Talk about it: What are your regrets?

Day 286:

Brainstorm small ways you can change things up. Sleep on different sides of the bed once a week, have breakfast in bed before work, take a half-day from work to do a fun activity, etc.

Day 287:

Is your friendship where you want it to be? What is great about it? What can you do to make it better?

Day 288:

Do you overreact? Pay attention to your thoughts. Are you making a big deal over something that doesn't require that much attention? Or could there possibly be an unmet need or an unaddressed issue that is making you sensitive to a certain topic? Reflect and share with each other.

Day 289:

Ask your partner: "What are your ideas about forgiveness?"

Day 290:

Acknowledge your partner's positive behaviors today.

Day 291:

Wwhat are your rules and boundaries with social media sites like Facebook, Instagram, and Twitter? For example, are exes allowed to be "friends" on Facebook?

Day 292:

Have you recently taken part in your own interests? Go solo or ask your partner to join you.

Day 293:

Unplug from social media and electronics for an agreed upon time today and tomorrow. Today, Partner 1 picks their preference for how the quality time will be spent.

Day 294:

Today, Partner 2 picks how the quality time will be spent. Still keep the electronics away!

———————— ❦ ————————

ANITA A. CHLIPALA, LMFT

128

Listening is an attitude of the heart, a genuine desire to be with another which both attracts and heals.

— J. Isham

Day 295:

When was your partner charming? Tell them.

Day 296:

Talk about it: What do you look forward to and/or dread the most when you get together with your own family?

Day 297:

What is your greatest accomplishment or success in life? Share with your partner.

Day 298:

If you put yourself down, imagine what you would say to your partner or friend on a similar issue. Apply this to yourself.

Day 299:

Change it up! Call or text your partner at a time when you normally wouldn't.

Day 300:

What do you do when one of you is sick? How do you help each other out? Would you like something more/different to happen?

Day 301:

Talk about it: What is your biggest phobia? Superstition?

Day 302:

Browse deal sites (such as Groupon, Vimbly, or LivingSocial) and plan a date on a budget!

Day 303:

If you call a time-out, call a time-in when you're both calm. Respect your partner's need for space if they need more time to self-soothe.

Day 304:

What is your life motto? Why? Share with your partner.

Day 305:

Do you know what exciting or stressful events your partner has coming up in their life? Check in. Does your partner need anything from you, such as encouraging words?

You can give without loving, but you can never love without giving.

— ROBERT LOUIS BALFOUR STEVENSON

Day 306:

Have knock-out, super-hot sex. Do whatever you need to do to make it special for each other.

Day 307:

Grade yourself. When your partner is being emotionally vulnerable with you, how well do you respond? How does your partner think you respond?

Day 308:

Share a memory of when your partner was tender.

Day 309:

Spend an extra 5–10 minutes helping your partner with an activity—cooking, chores, repairs, etc.

Day 310:

Talk about it: What is your favorite childhood tradition? Why?

Day 311:

It is critical for you to be happy and fulfilled in your own personal life—it will help you distinguish whether dissatisfaction comes from personal issues or relationship issues. How happy are you? Have you neglected any of your own needs?

Day 312:

Say this to your partner: "I love it when you _____."

Day 313:

Next time you want to make love to your partner but they turn you down, instead of taking it as a personal rejection, ask if there's something going on. Find out what is preventing them from being in the mood instead of assuming they do not want to be with you.

Day 314:

If you could relive one day with your partner, which day would it be? Tell them why.

Day 315:

Have a Potential Threat Check about your behavior: Do you "go too far" when you have had too much to drink? Do you signal availability by flirting or touching someone else? Where are your boundaries, and do they need to be adjusted?

—⋙∘⟨⟩∘⋘—

ANITA A. CHLIPALA, LMFT

Day 316:

Share with your partner your favorite thing that they did for you on a special occasion.

Day 317:

What does your partner gripe about that you do? Make an effort not to do it this week.

Day 318:

What was your parents' relationship like? What did you like about it? Dislike? Are any of these aspects present in your own relationship that you would like to have or eliminate?

Your emotional awareness and ability to handle feelings will determine your success and happiness in life.

— JOHN GOTTMAN

———⟡———

ANITA A. CHLIPALA, LMFT

Day 319:

Tell your partner how hot you find them. Pick one thing about their physical appearance that you love the most.

Day 320:

If you subject your partner to threats—whether outright or not—you will not be able to communicate effectively. Manage your emotions so you don't make threats that you don't mean or will regret.

Day 321:

Talk about it: How do you think free time should be spent? If your ideas are different, accept that your partner has a different preference, and make sure both of your preferences are taken into consideration.

Day 322:

Happiness is not something that happens to you. You create it. Optimize opportunities to increase your happiness. What can you do more of, do differently, or start doing in your life?

Day 323:

Do chores in lingerie and sexy boxers. If you have children, wear them under your clothes and tell your partner what they have to look forward to later that day.

Day 324:

If your partner sees that you are upset and asks how you're doing, don't say, "I'm fine" if you're not. You miss an opportunity to be in tune with each other. It's OK if you don't want to talk about it at that moment, but tell them that you aren't doing well but don't want to discuss it then. Revisit the discussion when you are emotionally ready.

Day 325:

Share with your partner an embarrassing moment.

Day 326:

Talk about it: If you could ink your partner when they're asleep, what tattoo would you give them? Why? Where?

Day 327:

Do your actions match your words consistently? You continually build trust when you do what you say you are going to do.

Day 328:

What is your favorite way that your partner flirts? Flirt in this way today!

Day 329:

Ｗhat event does your partner enjoy going to? Buy tickets for this.

Day 330:

Ｔell your partner: "I wish we had a better way of dealing with

_____."

Even after all this time the Sun never says to the Earth, "You owe me." Look what happens with a love like that. It lights the whole sky.

— HAFIZ

ANITA A. CHLIPALA, LMFT

Day 331:

Give your partner a small token of your love and appreciation.

Day 332:

What are your short- and long-term goals for your relationship? What do you both want in your relationship?

Day 333:

Spend time with your best friends.

Day 334:

Talk about it: When you die, how would you like to be remembered?

Day 335:

What are 3 things that you appreciate about today?

Day 336:

Make one of your partner's fantasies happen soon.

Day 337:

Talk about it: What traditions and rituals are important for special days like holidays?

Day 338:

Look for the positive in the negative. Your partner is probably not deliberately annoying you. How can you view an annoying trait or habit in a positive light? For example, if your partner is chronically late, you can catch up on email, read a book, or have some extra time for yourself.

—◦◦◦◦◦—

ANITA A. CHLIPALA, LMFT

$$\mathcal{D}ay\ 339:$$

S̶end your partner a loving text.

Let there be spaces in your togetherness.
— KAHLIL GIBRAN

Day 340:

You can choose your reactions. You may just need practice. Do you act before you think? Practice taking a few moments to think about what you want to say and do before you say and do it.

Day 341:

Talk about it: What worries you most about the future? What about your future together do you look forward to the most?

Day 342:

You reap the benefits when you treat your partner better. Have you recently been hurtful to your partner? Repair it with a kind gesture and a genuine "I'm sorry."

Day 343:

Do you blame your partner for the problems in your relationship? Take accountability for your relationship by examining your own role in these problems.

Day 344:

What is the most challenging part of your partner's day? Say or do one thing to make it better.

Day 345:

What inspires you about your partner? Tell them.

Day 346:

Don't expect your partner to be a mind reader. Be direct but gentle in your requests—and always ask instead of demanding.

Day 347:

Talk about it: What is the best part about being together?

Day 348:

Pick your battles. What is worth discussing? What can you let go?

Day 349:

Mail a card to your partner's workplace.

Day 350:

Talk about it: What people, places, or events make you most uncomfortable?

Love means to commit oneself without guarantee, to give oneself completely in the hope that our love will produce love in the loved person. Love is an act of faith, and whoever is of little faith is also of little love.

— ERICH FROMM

Day 351:

What's something you'd like to do with your partner that you've never done before? Share this with them and make it happen soon.

Day 352:

Show your partner—with your own flair and style—how much you appreciate them. Engage your creativity!

Day 353:

When was your partner generous without seeking a reward or recognition? Tell them.

Day 354:

Letting your partner feel romantically pursued can keep passion alive. Do one thing this week to make your partner feel pursued.

Day 355:

Talk about it: If you could be beamed anywhere in the universe, where would you want to go right now?

Day 356:

Have a 10-second kiss.

Day 357:

Get out of your typical routine. Do something, anything, differently today.

Day 358:

What do you look forward to about growing old? What scares you? Share with your partner.

Day 359:

Wake up or go to bed 15 minutes earlier to cuddle and talk in bed.

Day 360:

Talk about it: What do you appreciate about this time of your life?

My heart is ever at your service.

— WILLIAM SHAKESPEARE

—⟡—

ANITA A. CHLIPALA, LMFT

Day 361:

Do you feel like you are having enough fun in life and in your relationship? If not, what is missing?

Day 362:

Pull out a calendar for the next year. Decide what days you want to have relationship check-ins (minimum 2 dates). Things to consider: What are the best parts of your relationship? What is your level of personal happiness? Relationship satisfaction? Are needs being met? What would you like to see improved?

Day 363:

Do something that helps your partner or makes them happy without expecting anything in return.

—◦◦◦◦—

Day 364:

Talk about it: What was your favorite part of this book? What was your least favorite? What tips do you want to continue?

Day 365:

How has your relationship improved over the last 365 days? What would you like your relationship to look like in another 365 days? Share your thoughts and feelings with each other.

Made in the USA
Charleston, SC
03 January 2017